Keeping a Pony at Grass

© Mrs O. Faudel-Phillips 1958
2nd edition 1963, 3rd edition 1966
4th (revised) in paperback format 1985,
reprinted 1987. Redesigned and updated 2000

Edited and produced for The Pony Club
by Barbara Cooper

Designed and typeset by Alan Hamp
Photographs by Kit Houghton and David Wilshire

Published by The Pony Club
NAC Stoneleigh Park
Kenilworth, Warwickshire
CV8 2RW

Printed in Great Britain by Westway Offset, Wembley

ISBN 0-901366-71-4

Contents

List of Illustrations 4
Points of the Pony 6/7
Introduction 8

1   Wild Ponies   9
2   Fields   11
3   Feeding   27
4   Ponies in Frost and Snow   36
5   Feet and Shoes   37
6   Catching Up and Turning Out   41
7   Grooming   45
8   Care After Work   53
9   Stabling a Grass-kept Pony Overnight   56
10   Trimming, Washing, Clipping   58
11   The New Zealand Rug   64
12   Minor Ailments and First Aid   67
13   Companionship   75
14   Bringing in a Pony in Summer   76
15   Riding a Pony off Grass   77

Index   79

Illustrations

Points of the Pony 6/7

Fig.
1   New Forest ponies grazing in their native habitat. 9
2   Native breeds. Welsh mountain and Dartmoor ponies. 10
3   Suitable and unsuitable grasses for ponies. 12
4   Ponies in an over-grazed field. 13
5   Picking up droppings. 14
6   A neatly cut and trimmed hedge. 14
7   The most suitable type of water-trough. 15
8   An unsuitable water-trough. 15
9   A badly maintained gate. 16
10 A well-built post-and-rail fence. 17
11 Showing electrified fencing to a pony. 18
12 Badly neglected, dangerous fencing. 18
13 A permanent field-shelter with wide opening. 19
14 A field-shelter with too narrow an opening. 20
15 A portable field shelter. 20
16 A mare and foal sheltered by a high hedge. 21
17 Some poisonous plants. 22/3
18 A very small pony who needs only hay. 26
19a Diet chart. 28
19b Month-by-month feed chart. 29
20 Haynets for hunter, cob or pony, and very small pony. 31
21 The best way of storing feed. 33
22 A pony feeding from a portable manger. 33
23a Haynets correctly secured indoors and out. 34
23b An incorrectly positioned haynet. 35
24 New Forest pony in the snow. 36
25 A well-shod, well-cared for foot. 37
26 A foot with horn overgrowing the shoe. 38
27 A farrier removing a shoe and trimming horn. 38
28 Farrier's tools. 40

29 'A pony needs to be caught frequently.' 41
30 A correctly knotted halter. 42
31 A pony wearing a suitable headcollar. 43
32 'Never hustle a pony when turning him out.' 44
33 Grooming kit. 46
34 A pony tied up correctly. 47
35 A pony tied up incorrectly. 47
36 Equipment left in a dangerously kickable position. 48
37 Using a dandy brush. 49
38 Rubbing down a wet pony with straw. 50
39 A 'thatched' pony. 51
40 Washing a pony's tail. 52
41 Inspecting a pony's foot and shoe. 53
42 Knocking down risen clenches. 54
43 A good forelock. 59
44 A correctly banged tail. 60
45 Four types of trace-clip. 62
46 Stables set fair. 63
47 A pony wearing an outdoor (New Zealand) rug. 64
48 A hunter clip. 65
49 A pony wearing an indoor (stable-) rug. 66
50 A pony suffering from acute laminitis. 70
51 Cold-hosing a pony's sore feet. 74
52 Companionship. 75
53 'Keeping a pony at grass'. 78

Photographs
Kit Houghton: Figs. 1, 2, 3, 6, 8, 9, 10, 12, 13, 14, 17, 18, 22, 24, 25, 26, 27, 28, 29, 30, 32, 37, 38, 39, 40, 42, 43, 50, 53.
David Wilshire; Figs. 5, 7, 11, 16, 21, 23, 24, 31, 34, 35, 36, 42, 44, 46, 48, 49, 51.
Fig. 15 courtesy of Goodricks, York.
Line drawings
Maggie Raynor: Points of the Pony, pp 6/7. Figs. 20, 45, 47.
Carole Vincer: Figs. 3, 19.

Points of the Pony

(From Compass Pony Guide No.1)

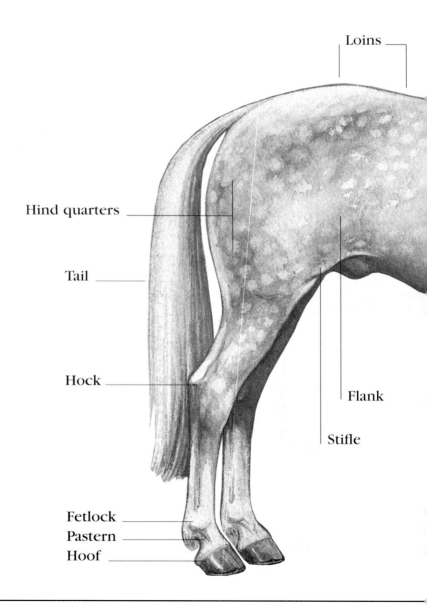

Loins

Hind quarters

Tail

Hock

Flank

Stifle

Fetlock

Pastern

Hoof

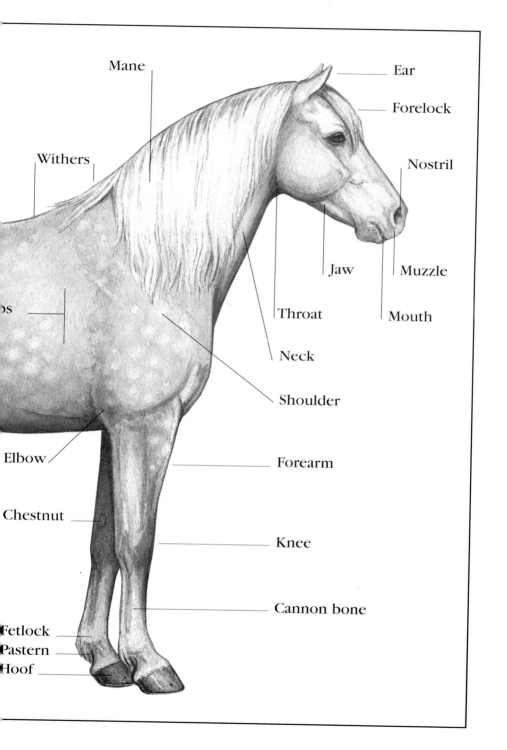

Mane

Ear

Forelock

Withers

Nostril

Jaw

Muzzle

Throat

Mouth

os

Neck

Shoulder

Elbow

Forearm

Chestnut

Knee

Cannon bone

Fetlock
Pastern
Hoof

Introduction

Wherever ponies at grass receive tender loving care and enjoy regular attention they will be happy and contented and will give of their best. How to achieve such a balanced state of affairs was in the mind of Olive Faudel-Phillips when she wrote this book.

When it comes to the understanding, handling, and managing of ponies as well as the responsibilities of riders and owners very little has changed over the years, whereas tack, equipment and feedstuffs have changed quite considerably. The text and illustrations of *Keeping a Pony at Grass* have therefore been updated where necessary.

The book explains how to keep a pony in good order throughout the year in safe and satisfactory surroundings. It also points out how to avoid the pitfalls. We hope that in its new Pony Club Paperback format it will continue to fulfil its purpose and to stand the test of time.

1
Wild Ponies

Ponies who have unlimited range – for example in the New Forest, on Dartmoor and on the Welsh Hills – may be able to live all the year round without human help *(figs. 1 & 2)*. They are in small herds in their natural surroundings, seeking water, food and shelter.

Their feet keep naturally trimmed by the wear they get. The grease in their ungroomed coats turns the rain, keeps them warm, and is a protection from flies.

On the other hand, a pony turned out in a field cannot live without regular attention all the year round. He has a large part of his freedom taken away. He can only drink and eat what he finds in that field. There may or may not be any shelter and, the range being restricted, his feet will not be naturally trimmed.

1 New Forest ponies in their native habitat

2 *Native breeds. (Above) Welsh mountain ponies on the Welsh hills.*
(Below) Dartmoor ponies grazing on moorland pasture.

2
Fields

Grazing

Grassland is a mixture of many different species of grass, clover, and other plants, which thrive or not, depending on the soil, altitude, rainfall and drainage.

In normal lowland country, ryegrass, cocksfoot and meadow fescue are the best species for grazing *(fig. 3)*. These do not thrive on hill land, where grasses such as fine-leaved fescues probably provide the best grazing value. A small percentage of certain weeds and grasses, such as dandelion, yarrow, and crested dogstail (much favoured by horses) play an important part in adding to the diet, thus avoiding monotony which horses dislike as much as humans.

Grass first begins to grow very slowly in April. It is at its best from mid-May to early July. By October the goodness has gone out of it and it has stopped growing.

Ponies will only graze the grasses which they like: they will starve rather than eat rank, tufty grass, or the sour grass around their own droppings. A pony therefore cannot live continually in the same field.

If constantly grazed or over-grazed *(fig. 4)* fields soon become 'horse-sick'. The ill effects of red worm are greatly increased in fields which are grazed too long without being properly dressed and rested. They must be left empty periodically and treated with nutrients.

If ponies start gnawing bark off trees it is a sign that something is lacking in their diet. By always keeping a large lump of rock salt in the field the risk of ponies stripping the bark will be lessened.

Maintenance

Where grassland has greatly deteriorated it may be quicker and better to plough and re-seed or to re-seed partially: i.e. to work in a grass seed mixture, while drastically harrowing to remove the dead grasses. There are a number of selective sprays which kill off the weeds, but if possible they should be avoided, for as already mentioned, weeds in the right proportion add valuable variety to the pasture.

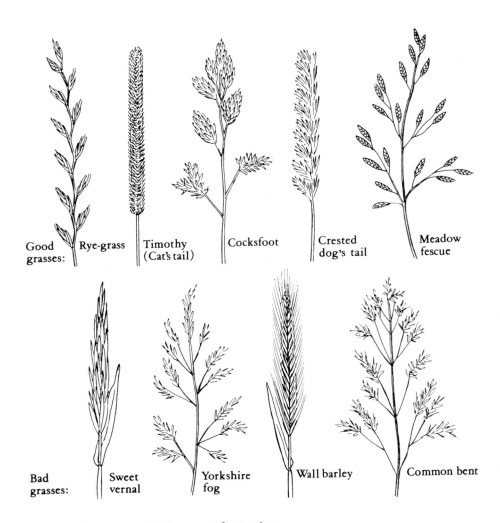

Good grasses: Rye-grass | Timothy (Cat's tail) | Cocksfoot | Crested dog's tail | Meadow fescue

Bad grasses: Sweet vernal | Yorkshire fog | Wall barley | Common bent

3 Suitable and unsuitable grasses for ponies.

The management of grazing is a fascinating subject very well covered in a variety of publications. Basically the best results are achieved by improving the soil with the right fertilisers; having cattle or sheep to share the fields from time to time; or cutting at regular intervals the grasses that the ponies do not eat. Fields should be grazed well but not too severely, with periods of rest and regular harrowing in the early spring.

Care of Grass
Sharing a Field with Cattle or Sheep. This is one of the best ways of

keeping a field evenly grazed and the grass sweet. The cattle will pull off the rough, longer grasses.

Having two fields is ideal. Each field can then be rested in turn and receive correct treatment.

Electric fencing as a temporary measure in the spring enables a field to be grazed evenly by giving the grass in the rested part a chance to grow. (See pp. 17 and 18.)

Droppings

Horse and pony droppings should be regularly picked up from any field *(fig.5)*. Using a pair of boards or a small shovel and wheelbarrow, take the droppings away to a manure heap or garden compost heap. If it is not possible to pick up the droppings regularly they must be scattered with a wire rake once a week.

Fields need attention at certain seasons, year in and year out, so seek the advice of a neighbouring farmer about how to care for your field; when to harrow and roll; when and with what to dress the field; when to have a cutter run over the field to keep down thistles, long weeds and rough rank grasses; when and how to cut and trim the hedges *(fig. 6)* and to cut brambles and nettles.

It is worth taking a little trouble and care so that your pony can get the best grazing out of every part of a field.

4 Ponies in an over-grazed field.

5 *Picking up droppings.*

6 *A neatly cut and trimmed hedge.*

Water

It is essential for ponies to have a plentiful supply of clean water so that they can drink as and when they want. The most natural and the best is a running stream or a pond with a spring in it. A stagnant pond clogged with mud and weeds does not provide a good water supply. If deeply silted it will be dangerous, and should therefore be fenced off to prevent ponies getting stuck in it.

Some fields have piped water and troughs *(fig. 7)*. It is wiser to have one of the cattle troughs which are specially fitted with a ballcock so that each time ponies or cattle drink, the trough automatically refills itself. The ballcock is enclosed in its own covered box so that animals

7 The most suitable type of water-trough.

8 An unsuitable water-trough.

cannot interfere with it. Even so, it must be looked at once a week. Grit or weeds may get in, causing it to choke and flood. Or something may be wrong with the water supply, which prevents the trough from filling properly.

Avoid using an old bath or water-tank for a trough *(fig. 8)*; unfortunately they are too often seen in fields. They spoil the look of a field, and the sharp sides can give a pony a nasty cut or bruise.

If there is no water supply in the field, water has to be taken daily by hand. The amount that a pony will drink in a day varies from three to eight gallons, depending on conditions, weather, amount of moisture in the grass, etc.

Whatever container is used must be firmly placed so that the pony cannot knock it over when it is half empty. All troughs should be emptied and scrubbed out at least four times a year.

Gates
All gates **must** open wide, shut properly, and have a secure catch. Gates tied up with string *(fig. 9)* or looped round with wire are not signs of good horsemastership and show that you don't care much whether your pony gets out or strays on a road.

9 A badly maintained gate: off its hinges and tied with string. At centre: a wire mesh fence, poorly constructed and unsuitable for ponies.

10 A well-built post-and-rail fence.

There is a simple inexpensive galvanised non-sag gate-hook on the market which the cleverest pony will not be able to undo.

Fences

A post and rail is the best fence and is the right kind of artificial fencing for horses and ponies *(fig. 10)*. Although it is very expensive, it is safe, and it lasts for years. Posts and wire are more often used, but do not last so long. This is a cheap form of fencing and acceptable only while the wire is taut and the posts firm. It must be regularly inspected and kept in good repair. An alternative is the wire/plastic top rail which is less liable to injure a pony and is considerably cheaper than timber.

Permanent electric fencing, with tape or rope, is very cost-effective, highly visible, and greatly respected by horses and ponies. Be sure to lead them up and show it to them the first time it is used *(fig. 11)*.

Barbed wire is *always* dangerous, particularly if it is not taut. *Old* wire fences are also a hazard *(fig. 12)*.

Hedges, walls and banks, which provide various kinds of natural fencing in different parts of the country, are all good if maintained. There must be no weak places for ponies to push through. Gaps mended with bits of wire, a single thin rail, or dead branches, will soon become gaps

11 *Showing electrified fencing to a pony.*

12 *Badly neglected, dangerous fencing.*

again. In spring and autumn, when ponies are changing their coats, they will rub against any convenient post, rail or gate.

Inspect all fences regularly.

Shelter

This is essential: in winter from rain and wind and in summer from sun and flies. It can be a building or a shed, a high stout hedge or shady trees.

An open-fronted shed *(fig. 13)* is good. A shed with only one doorway or with narrow doorways *(fig. 14)* is bad, because two ponies going out quickly may get squeezed, and ponies' hips are easily injured. Many a pony is shy and afraid of being kicked or bullied by another pony. He will not use a shed unless it has a wide open front, i.e. three sides closed and a good part of the fourth side open.

Portable shelters *(fig. 15)* are becoming more and more popular. One of their advantages is that they do not require Planning Permission.

It is often noticed that some ponies will not use their shed during the worst winter weather, but in summer, when it is hot and the flies drive them nearly mad, they will take refuge.

Ponies rarely lie down in their shed, under trees, or close to a hedge. More often they will take advantage of a slight fold in the ground, which gives shelter from wind when they are lying down.

13 *A permanent field shelter with suitably wide opening.*

14 An unsuitable field-shelter – uncared-for and with too narrow an opening.

15 A portable wooden field shelter.

A high, deep and stout hedge *(fig. 16)* is good and gives shelter in all weathers, as well as acting as a wind break. Banks and walls protect from rain and wind but not always from the sun.

In summer, shady trees give protection from sun and flies, and ponies will stand under them, usually head to tail. In winter, trees without their leaves do not offer much protection. Small thickets, bushy hollies, clumps of non-poisonous evergreen shrubs or a small wood or spinney are all places where ponies can shelter in rough weather.

Inspection

Fields must be regularly and thoroughly inspected all over the grass and along fences. Look out for bottles, tins and litter. Check wire fences. They may have been climbed through and the wire loosened. There may even be pieces of wire lying around.

Look out for any holes. Fill them in with stones and earth, and stamp them well down.

Old dead branches sticking out at eye level can be dangerous and should be broken or sawn off close to the trunk. In fact it is essential to develop the habit of noticing anything in a field that may cause a pony to get hurt or caught up.

16 A mare and foal sheltered by a high hedge.

(a) Ragwort

(b) Yew

c)

17a,b,c Some poisonous plants: Ragwort (opposite, top);Yew (opposite, below);
Deadly Nightshade (above).

Look around the field and hedges for poisonous plants, such as deadly nightshade *(fig. 17c)* and ragwort *(fig. 17a)*. Pull them up by the
roots. Remove them from the field, and burn them. Also, beware of yew
(fig. 17b) – particularly half-dead branches and twigs. Yew is deadly
poisonous to horses and cattle.

scientifically controlled to provide a correctly balanced diet.

If, for various reasons, you can only give one kind of extra food, then give the pony hay. Plenty of really good, sweet-smelling hay, and you will not go far wrong.

It is wiser not to give oats, beans or maize to very small ponies *(fig. 18)*; they usually do well on hay alone. If they must be given a short feed, give them pony cubes.

The same applies to extra food for an excitable, hot pony. Good rarely comes of cutting out his food altogether, and the pony will only lose condition. Give him cubes and plenty of hay. In both cases feed 'Pony ' grade of any of the proprietary brands of cube. Do not buy a whole winter's supply in one go, as they will deteriorate.

Quantities of Feed Required

This information is taken from *The Manual of Horsemanship*. The guidelines provided are based on the following work levels:

• *Maintenance.* The horse is able to remain healthy and to maintain all bodily functions, such as eating, breathing, keeping, warm, growing a summer or winter coat, or repairing any injuries.

18 A very small pony usually does well on hay.

Any working horse or pony who is put out to grass for a break from routine work will be living at maintenance level.

•*Light Work.* Maintenance plus up to one hour's hacking daily, mostly walking and trotting. Very little cantering.

•*Medium Work.* Maintenance plus an average of one-and-a-half hour's hacking daily, with active work which might include cantering, jumping, Pony Club rallies and competing at shows.

•*Hard Work.* Maintenance plus final fitness programme for participating in:

Pony Club Camp

Polo

Hunting

Regular Mounted Games Team Training

One Day Horse Trials

Long Distance Training

GUIDELINES FOR A 12hh PONY

Capacity 7.5kgs (16½ lb) per day.

Work Level:

•*Maintenance*. The pony requires only good grass and/or hay (bulk feed).

•*Light Work.* The pony requires only good grass and/or hay.

•*Medium Work.* 15% of the bulk feed may be replaced by concentrates (pony cubes – beware of oats): i.e. 1kg (approximately 2¼ lbs), divided into one or two feeds a day.

•*Hard Work.* Up to 30% of the bulk feed may be replaced by concentrates: i.e. approx. 2kgs (4½ lbs), divided into two or three feeds per day.

GUIDELINES FOR A 14hh PONY

Capacity 9.3kgs (20½ lbs) per day. Depending, on the temperament, behaviour and fitness of the pony, the amount and type of concentrates may need adjusting (*see figs. 19a and b*).

Work Level:

•*Maintenance.* The pony requires only good grass and/or hay.

•*Light Work.* 10% to 15% of the bulk feed may be replaced with concentrates: i.e. 1 to 1.5kgs (2 to 3¼ lbs) divided into one or two feeds per day.

•*Medium Work.* Up to 25% concentrates in the diet: that is, up to 2.25kgs (5 lbs) divided into two or three feeds per day.

•*Hard Work.* Up to 33.3% concentrates in the diet: i.e. up to 3kgs (6¾ lbs) in three or four feeds per day.

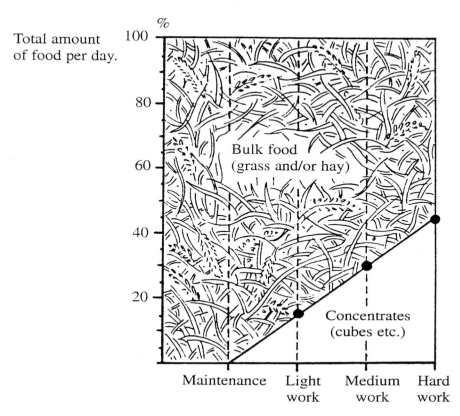

Total amount of food per day.

19a Chart showing diet related to work for a pony of approximately 14.2hh (148cm).

When to feed

The best time to give food to ponies at grass is early in the morning and again about an hour before dusk. Some hay should also be given early in the morning, and the rest of the hay and short feed in the afternoon. In this way the pony will get the best advantage from the food during the coldest part of the twenty-four hours.

These times are not always possible but make sure that the pony is fed at the same time every day. THIS IS IMPORTANT. All animals respond to regular hours and seem to have an in-built clock in their heads. The pony will be waiting at the gate. If two or more ponies are turned out together they will soon begin milling around, and trouble will start if they are kept waiting . So always feed at regular times every day.

Some people occasionally give extra feed or they may do so only – if the pony is being ridden or worked. This may be all right when there is enough grass, but in winter is is both unfair and bad for a pony, who

19b **Month-by-Month Feed Chart**

	Hay in kilos (pounds)			Coarse Mix or Pony Cubes in kilos (pounds)		
	14.2h (148cm)	12-14h (121.8-142.2)	11h or under (111.7)	14.2 (148cm)	12-14h (121.8-142.2)	11h or under (111.7)
January	8-9 (18-20)	7-8 (16-18)	5-6½ (12-15)	2 (5) or more	1½ (3) or more	1 (2) or more
February	8-9 (18-20)	7-8 (16-18)	5-6½ (12-15)	2¼ (5) or more	1½ (3) or more	1 (2) or more
March	8-9 (18-20)	7-8 (16-18)	5-6½ (12-15)	1¾ (4) or more	1 (2) or more	½ (1) or more
April	6-6½ (14-15)	4½-5½ (10-12)	3½ (8)	1¾ (4) or more	1 (2) or more	½ (1) or more
May	—	—	—	—	—	—
June	—	—	—	—	—	
July	—	—	—	1¾ (4) or more if working hard	1 (2) or more if working hard	½ (1) or more if working hard
August	—	—	—			
September	—	—	—			
October	4½ (10)	3½ (8)	4½ (5)	1 (2) or more	½ (1) or more	¼ (½) or more
November	6½ (15)	4½ (10)	3½ (8)	1½ (3) or more	1 (2) or more	½ (1) or more
December	8-9 (18-20)	7-8 (16-18)	5-6½ (12-15)	2¼ (5) or more	2¼ (5) or more	1 (2) or more

cannot understand why he is being fed one day and not the next. When the pony needs extra food, feed him regularly and consistently.

Let us consider the four seasons of a year and pick out the months in which ponies need, and do not need, extra food. This will depend on a number of factors the pony himself, the field that he lives in, the work that he is doing, the weather, and the area in which he lives – north or south, east or west, town or country.

May and June. The grass is growing and has its full feed value. Ponies can eat all the food and bulk that they need. They can also make good the condition they have lost during the winter and the earlier months of the year. A pony should fill out and get a gloss on his coat. He should be given the chance to pick up, and should not be worked if in poor condition. He should not need any extra food.

July to November. On average grazing, a pony should be able to live without extra feeding except during the holidays. For an average summer holiday programme he will need a short feed daily. He will work many days with long hours out of his field, and the concentrated short feed will keep him going during those hours. He will catch up with his bulk food because he can graze during most summer nights.

November to Mid-December. Unless on very good grazing, a pony will need hay once a day. If being hunted or worked hard he will also need a short feed daily.

Mid-December to April. Ponies must now be fed hay once or twice daily: definitely twice daily during frost or snow. If a pony is hunted or worked hard he must have a daily short feed as well as hay.
Thinking ahead as you must always do with the care and feeding of animals, the pony must be fit and well in time for Easter (often one of the busiest holiday seasons) so give a good short feed as well as hay daily from December to April. As winter turns to spring, ponies feel at their lowest. They have used up all their surplus fat. They will soon be changing their coats. The grass has not begun to grow, so that daily extra short feed will really help them.

Haynets are usually in three sizes *(fig. 20)*:
Large: (Hunter) holding 10 to 12 lbs (4½-5½ kilos) of hay when stuffed *completely* full.
Medium: (Cob and Pony) 7 to 8 lbs (3-3½ kilos)of hay when *completely* stuffed full.

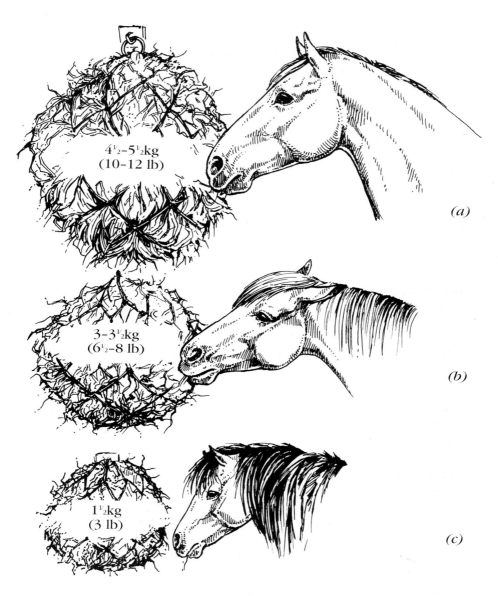

4½–5½kg
(10–12 lb)

(a)

3–3½kg
(6½–8 lb)

(b)

1½kg
(3 lb)

(c)

20 *Haynets with correct amounts of hay for (a) hunter, (b) cob or pony, and (c) very small pony.*

Small: (Very Small Ponies) up to 3 lbs (1½ kilos) of hay when stuffed *completely* full.

Buy tarred haynets – they last much longer. And remember that hay from the bale must be shaken out before it is stuffed into the net.

31

Hay. Budget for the quantity needed for the winter and allow a margin in case there is a long frost or the pony needs extra hay.

A pony eating two medium-sized nets of hay a day will need one ton of good hay for 18 to 20 weeks. If the hay is of moderate quality more will be needed. Uneaten, stale or damp hay left in the net must be taken out and thrown away.

Short feed. How to budget for quantities:

A pony having about 4 lbs (1¾ kilos) a day of either pony cubes or coarse mix, will need two 25-kilo bags a month.

If a big double handful of chaff is mixed with each feed, allow two large sacks of chaff a month.

If 1½ to 2 lb (½ to ¾ kilo) of bran are used instead of chaff, allow 25 kilos of bran a month.

From these quantities it should be easy to work out approximately how much food will be needed and what will be the cost of the pony's keep.

Ponies, like humans, vary in how much and what they eat, and no rule can be laid down. Observe the pony and learn from your observations.

Storage

All forage must be stored in a clean dry place, free from rats and out of bounds to chickens, dogs, etc. Large bins with lids *(fig. 21)* are best for storing pony cubes, coarse mix etc. Do not use wooden containers which are chewable.

When stored, cubes and coarse mix may deteriorate and lose protein value, so don't store a whole winter's supply.

If the field where the pony is turned out is some distance from the house it may be necessary to have a dry place near by, in which to store hay and feed.

How to Give Short Feed. It is wasteful to throw a feed down on the bare ground, especially in wet weather, when a container must be provided. Portable managers made of polyurethane, which can be hooked over a rail *(fig. 22)* are very practical. Alternatives are containers made of wood or galvanised iron. Each pony should have his own, placed wide apart and out of kicking range. If you use a home-made container make sure that it is very strong and that there are no splinters.

If one pony has to have a special feed or an extra feed he should be taken from the field, out of sight of the other ponies, to be fed.

21 *The best way of storing feed: in large bins with hinged, securable lids.*

22 *A pony feeding from a portable manger.*

33

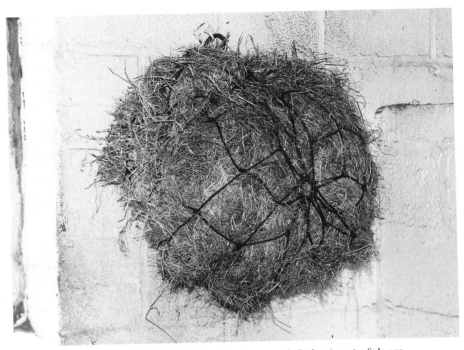

23a Haynets correctly secured (above) indoors and (below) out of doors.

23b An incorrectly positioned haynet, with the hay too loosely packed.

How to Give Hay

It is wasteful to put hay on the ground: ponies pick out the best pieces, treading and spoiling the rest. However, if there are a number of ponies turned together this may be the only way – in which case be sure to put the heaps in a big circle, each heap wide apart from the last so that ponies cannot kick each other. Put one heap extra to the number of ponies. There will be less squabbling and it ensures that a shy pony will get his fair share.

Hay fed in haynets is excellent; any not eaten will remain clean and above the muddy ground. The ponies are able to return and eat when they want to. There must be a haynet for each pony in the field. Haynets must be tied very firmly to a strong fence *(fig. 23a)* or tree, and high enough so that the pony does not catch a foot in it *(fig. 23b)*. A haynet sags lower as it empties. Place haynets well apart to prevent biting and kicking.

In wet weather the ground will get poached wherever ponies are fed, so it may be necessary to use different parts of a field or fence if this is practical.

4
Ponies in Frost and Snow

The water supply, whether trough or pond, must have the ice broken at least three times a day. A pony is unable to break even thin ice by himself.

Additional hay must be given during frost or snow, when grazing is not possible. Ponies do not necessarily mind very cold, dry weather; what they hate is cold, wet weather and wind.

It is very important to go on feeding when the thaw sets in, as it is often wet and cold; the grass that exists is soggy and shrivelled.

Frozen ground has no give in it and is very rough for an unshod pony. The horn may crack and bits may break off. If the ponies are shod this may not happen. In either case, when the thaw sets in look out for bruised soles or heels.

Before riding a pony in snow, smear thick grease, such as *Vaseline,* on the soles and frogs of all four feet to prevent the snow from 'balling'.

24 New Forest pony in the snow.

5
Feet and Shoes

'No foot, no 'oss' – Mr. Jorrocks has handed down to us no truer words and we shall do well never to forget them. A pony with feet and shoes regularly cared for *(fig. 25)* will go a long way to giving one hundred per cent performance. It is neither safe nor fair on a pony to ride him when his feet or shoes need attention.

Pain and discomfort will be caused by overgrown, split and cracked horn; worn, loose or twisted shoes; risen clenches; horn growing over the shoes, and the shoe pressing into the foot or heels *(fig. 26)*. These may also cause brushing, faulty action, stumbling and bruising. So it is important for ponies – from the time that they are foals and for the rest

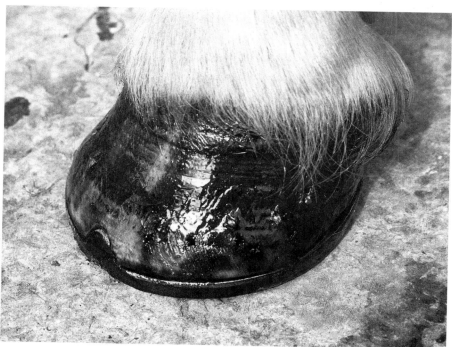

25 *A well-shod, well-cared for foot.*

26 (above) A foot with horn overgrowing the shoe.
27a (opposite, above) A farrier removing a shoe.
27b (opposite, below) A farrier trimming horn.

of their lives – to be taken to or visited by the farrier every four to six weeks: that is, eight to thirteen times a year *(fig. 27a)*.

This does not necessarily mean a new set of shoes at each visit. The amount of road work and the pony's conformation and action are what govern the length of time that a set of shoes will last.

The farrier may take off the shoes, re-shape them, trim the feet and put the shoes on again with new nails. This is called a 'refit' or, by some people, a 'remove'.

If a pony is unshod, the farrier will trim the horn to keep the foot a good shape and the right length *(fig. 27b)*.

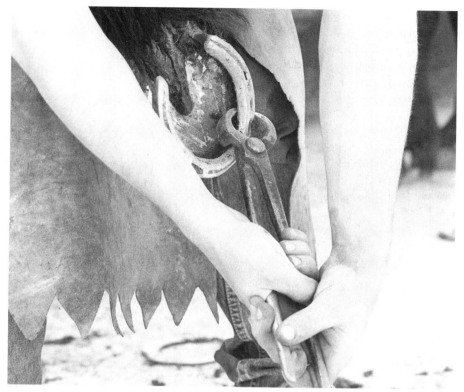

(a)

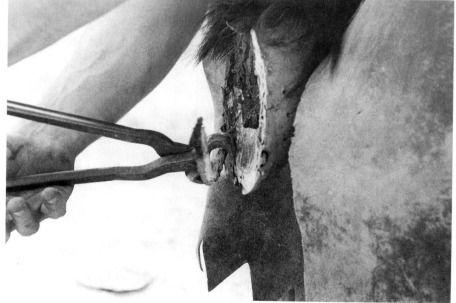

(b)

If a pony is not going to be ridden during term time it is wise to ask the farrier for his advice before the holidays are over. He may refit the front shoes and leave the hind feet unshod.The front shoes prevent the toes from cracking.

If you are at boarding school, arrangements must be made with the farrier to attend to the pony's feet at least once during term time, whether the shoes are left on or taken off.

In *The Manual of Horsemanship* (Chapter 21) there are full details and a good deal of useful information on feet, shoes and shoeing.

28 Farrier's tools:(above) for forging (below) for shoeing.

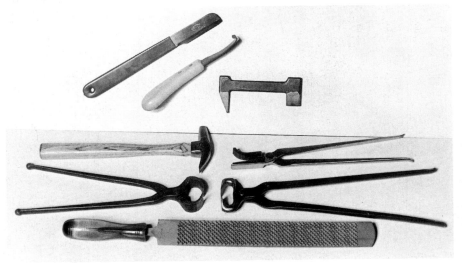

6
Catching Up and Turning Out

Ponies need to be caught frequently *(fig. 29)*. Some are never difficult to catch; others remain shy all their lives. There is many a pony who will not let a grown-up catch him. Young or shy ponies prefer to be gently scratched or rubbed on the shoulder or neck, rather than patted. Coax a shy pony into the habit of coming to a call, letting him link up the voice with a tit-bit. On each visit to the field, slip a piece of rope or string around the pony's neck, whether you intend to catch him or not, and make much of him for a few moments. Allow plenty of time – ponies can sense when anyone is in a hurry. They hate to be hustled.

29 *'A pony needs to be caught frequently.'*

30 A correctly knotted halter.

A halter is better than a headcollar for catching up and turning out *(fig, 30)*. Before putting on or taking off the halter, always slip the rope around the neck behind the pony's ears, so that there is something to hold the pony by if he moves while the halter is being adjusted or removed.

It may be necessary, as a temporary measure, to leave a headcollar *(fig. 31)* on a pony at grass. It should be made of leather, not of synthetic material. (If the pony is in trouble, leather will break, but nylon, for example, will not.)It must be fitted very carefully. It should allow a width of three fingers anywhere around the nose so that there

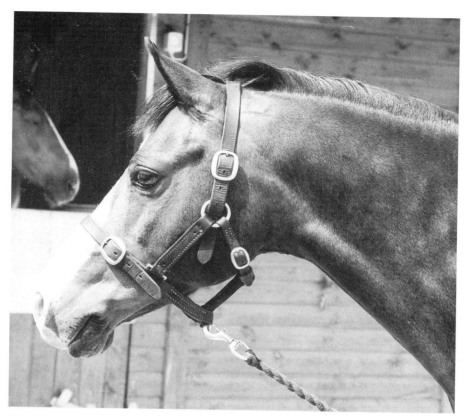

*31 A pony wearing a correctly fitted headcollar. Note that the clip on the lead-rope
is towards the pony's chest.*

is ample room for the jaws to move freely when the pony eats. The
headcollar must be kept well oiled and soft, to prevent chafing. Reasons
against turning a pony out in a headcollar are that he may get caught
when rubbing against a tree or post, or he might catch the heel of a
shoe in the leather when scratching his head with a hind foot.

Turning a Pony Out

If a pony is turned out incorrectly he will often be difficult to catch up
again. **Never** hustle a pony when turning him out *(fig. 32)*. Letting him
gallop away immediately causes harm and may make him excitable
when being turned out or caught up. Try to leave him before he moves.
It is the last impression left on the pony's mind that counts.

If care is taken each time, most ponies will soon learn the simple
drill. Shut the gate and lead the pony at least ten yards into the field.
Turn him round and face the gate. Stand still. Pat him. Take off his

32 'Never hustle a pony when turning him out.'

halter. Pat him again, and walk right away. If he must have a tit-bit give it to him just before you walk away.

The reason for turning him to face the gate is that if he gallops away and kicks, you can get out of the way as he turns.

If more than one pony is being turned out, keep them well apart and arrange to let them loose at the same moment.

7
Grooming

Equipment that you will need *(fig. 33):*
Halter
Bucket quarter full of cold water
Sponge
Hoof pick
Water brush
Dandy brush
Body brush
Curry comb
Stable rubber
Sweat scraper
Hoof oil and brush
Sweat rug or sacking ⎤
Surcingle or roller ⎦ if pony is wet
Also:
Bundle of straw or hay
Set of stable bandages
Tail bandage.

The point of grooming a pony at grass is to make him clean and tidy for the day's work. *Little or no grease should be removed as this is the pony's protection against sun, flies, rain and wind.* In contrast a stabled pony, who is confined, is groomed to get out all grease, to keep him really clean and healthy and to tone up his muscles and circulation.

All healthy ponies at grass have a good natural shine on their coats. When they change their coats twice a year, in spring and autumn, they do not need to be brushed too much. Nature's way is to shed a little then grow a little.

Whether a pony is being groomed in the field, near the house, or in a shed or box, he must be tied up correctly to something firm but safe, such as a wall *(fig. 34), not* to a vehicle *(fig. 35)* or near kickable items *(fig. 36)*. Remember to use a quick-release knot, as in *figure 34.*

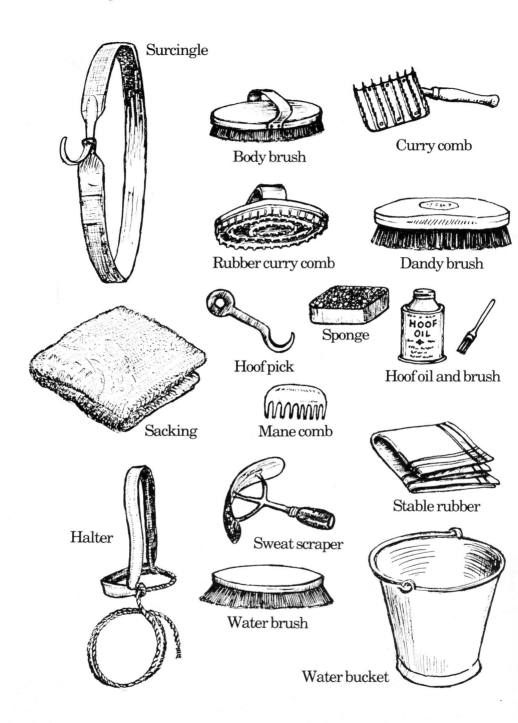

Surcingle

Body brush

Curry comb

Rubber curry comb

Dandy brush

Sacking

Hoof pick

Sponge

Hoof oil and brush

Mane comb

Stable rubber

Halter

Sweat scraper

Water brush

Water bucket

33 Grooming kit.

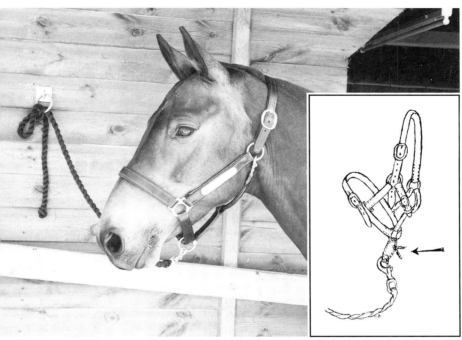

34 A pony tied up correctly. Note the quick-release knot. Between the cheekpiece ring and the rope-clip there should be a small loop of string (arrowed in inset at right) which will break in an emergency

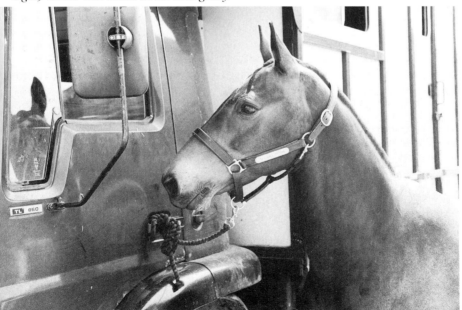

35 Never tie a pony like this.

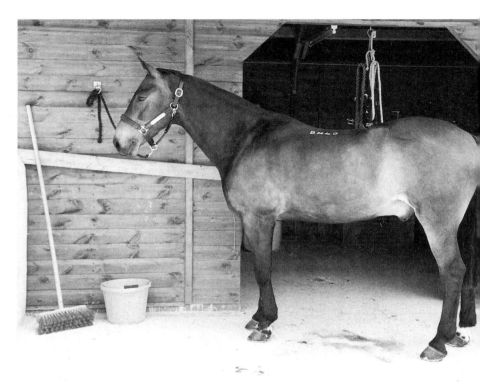

36 Never leave equipment near a pony who is tied up.

Grooming a Dry Pony

Sponge the eyes, the nose, and under the tail if necessary. (If overdone this removes too much natural grease.) Pick out each foot. Using a water brush, wash each foot, getting off the dry mud and dirt; there are two reasons for this – to enable the feet and shoes to be properly inspected, and for good appearance. Horn caked with old mud under a clean pony and tack spoils the turnout. Remember also that if you apply oil to hooves that are not clean and dry, moisture and dirt can be trapped under it, causing decay. So, even if the pony is likely to get muddy again soon, wash his feet and try not to slosh water over the joints and pasterns. Practice makes for speed and skill

Use a dandy brush *(fig. 37)* or rubber curry comb to remove the mud from the body and legs. All the parts where the saddle, girth, martingale and bridle touch must be quite free from mud and dirt.

Use a body brush for the mane and tail and brush them both thoroughly. A dandy brush and comb will damage the hairs of the mane and tail. (The only time to use a comb is when plaiting or trimming). Putting on a tail bandage is optional, depending on how soon the pony is going to be ridden. Remember to wet the tail only. Never wet the bandage, because it will shrink as it dries and tighten around the dock, sometimes stopping the circulation. Wipe the whole pony over in the direction of the hair with a rubber. Oil the feet, being careful to do all round the horn and across the bulbs of the heels.

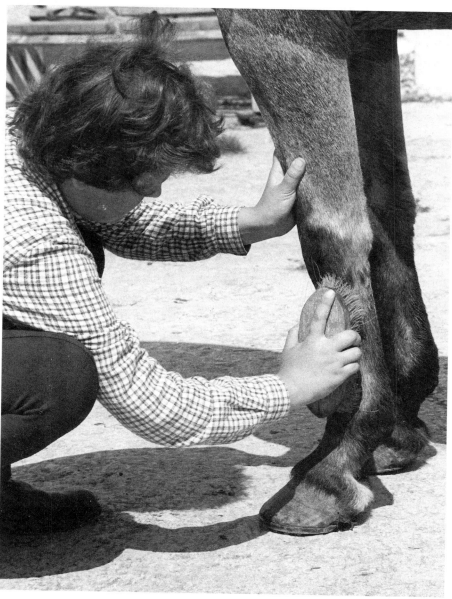

37 Using a dandy brush correctly.

Grooming a Wet Pony

Use a sweat scraper to get off the worst of the wet on the neck and body.

With a good handful of straw or hay rub the pony down, removing as much water as possible *(fig. 38)*.

Never rub **against** the coat: this only makes the wet permeate through to the skin. Always rub the way in which the coat lies.

A saddle must not be put on a wet back, so to get the pony really dry, lay some fresh straw or hay all over his back and loins. Put on a sweat rug to keep the straw in place, then strap on a surcingle or roller to prevent the rug and straw from slipping off *(fig. 39)*.

With a rubber, dry the ears throughly. If they are cold, 'pull' them.

Groom the feet as for a dry pony.

Rub down the legs and pasterns with a handful of straw or hay. If they are very muddy, put on loosely a set of stable bandages, with hay, straw, cotton wool or gamgee underneath. The legs will dry quickly. Later the dry mud can be brushed off with a dandy brush.

Groom the mane and tail, even if they are wet. Wash the tail if it is muddy *(fig. 40)*.

38 Rubbing down a wet pony with straw.

39 A 'thatched' pony.

Give the pony some water and some hay or feed, and leave him with the straw and sweat rug or sacking on for about an hour, when he should be dry enough to have any mud brushed off and for you to complete the grooming.

Do not leave a pony thatched with straw for much longer than an hour because he may become too hot and start to sweat and get itchy.

A sweat rug and sacking placed directly on top of a wet back will not dry it. Everything will just stay clammy and wet, and the pony may catch cold. Putting straw under a sweat rug or sacking allows the steam and damp air to get away, so that the pony dries off.

If you prefer modern methods, there are excellent rugs on the market which absorb moisture and allow it to pass through the material, leaving the pony dry underneath.

It is important, whether grooming a wet or dry pony, always to look him over for any hurt and to inspect his feet and shoes.

40 Wash the tail if it is muddy.

8

Care after Work

After a Short Ride

Ponies like to get back to their field after being worked. On the other hand, after an ordinary ride it does a **dry** pony no harm to put him in a stable. During the summer he may be kept in for part of the day because of the flies.

Whichever is being done, give the pony a chance to stale, then brush off the saddle mark and look the pony over for any hurt. Inspect the feet and shoes *(fig.41)*.

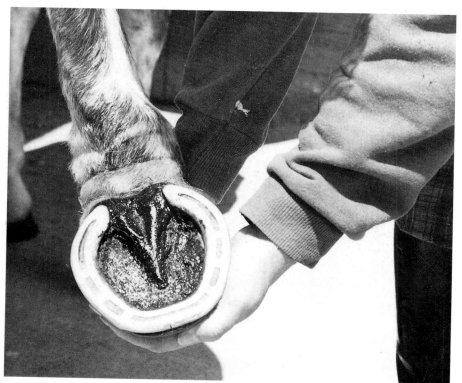

41 The correct way of holding a pony's foot in order to check the sole and shoe.

After a Long Day

The occasions on which a pony must be put straight out into the field are after hunting, after a long day, or if he is wet with either rain or sweat. At any of these times, whether in summer or winter, a grass-kept pony should not be put in a stable, but should be taken into his field as soon as possible. These are not the times to dawdle and talk but to get on with doing what is necessary for the pony.

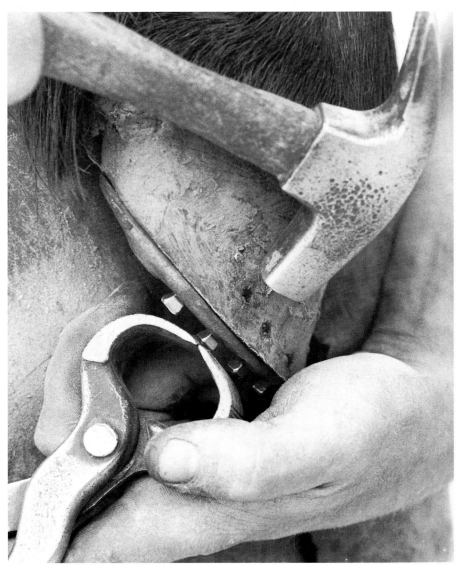

42 A farrier tidying up clenches.

Take off the saddle and bridle and put on a halter. Give the pony a chance to stale. Rub the saddle mark and behind the ears briskly with a handful of straw or hay, to restore the circulation.

In winter offer some tepid or slightly warm water, but do not worry or hang about waiting if the pony will not touch it.

Take a quick look over him for any hurt – and then turn him out right away. Even if it is pelting with rain or blowing a gale most ponies lie down and roll at once, have a good shake, pull a few mouthfuls of grass, go for a short trot, and then have a drink. This is nature's way of easing tired muscles, warming a pony up, or drying him off, if he is sweating.

Treating a pony in this way will keep his feet, legs and wind right, and will prevent chills and colds.

If left in his stable when sweating, damp or wet, a pony cannot move around enough to keep himself warm and so is very likely to catch a chill while drying off.

If it is winter, the pony's feed and hay should be put out into its usual place in the field.

The Day after a Long Day

Without fail the following day the pony must be caught up and carefully looked over for cuts, thorns, sore mouth, back and girth galls or hurt of any sort. Brush off any remaining sweat marks.

Pick out and inspect the feet and shoes. There may be one or more clenches up *(fig. 42)*, or a loose or twisted shoe. Trot the pony up in hand on a road or on a level piece of hard ground, to test for lameness.

Check that he ate up his feed.

Turn him out again straight away, giving hay and feed as usual.
The pony will be better out in the field rather than in a stable, except in summer if the flies are bad.

Whether summer or winter, it is only fair to the pony **not** to ride him the day after a hard or long day.

9

Stabling a Grass-Kept Pony Overnight

In very wet weather it is sometimes convenient to catch up the pony the night before a day's work.

He must be thoroughly dried, his feet picked out and washed, and his mane and tail brushed. Follow the full details as for grooming a wet pony.

In the box there must be a good bed of straw or other bedding, a bucket full of water, a feed and some hay.

The top door of the box should be left open so that there is plenty of air. If the window is on the same side as the door it also should be open. Avoid cross- draught.

No matter what the weather, ponies do not catch cold out of doors. But once you bring them into a stable without plenty of air they may catch cold.

When the pony is quite dry it is all right to put on a thin lightweight rug with crossed surcingles or a roller; an unlined jute or even a summer sheet is enough. For some ponies, covering over the back and loins is advisable. Because a pony has a thick coat it does not mean that he will not feel cold in a stable. A pony in a field is not cold, because he can move about freely and there are no draughts, whereas a pony in a stable (say 10x12ft, 3x3·7m) is unable to move about enough to keep his circulation going. Nor can he get away from a draught – which he will feel but you may not be aware of. As with anything connected with an animal, no hard and fast rule applies. Ponies vary, and every stable is different.

How to Know and What to Do if the Pony is too Hot or too Cold
When a pony has stood in for, say, a couple of hours – if his ears are cold and his coat is staring, it means that he is cold.

If he is sweating and his ears are cold he has broken out into a cold sweat and is cold.

If he is sweating and his ears are hot, and if the box feels fuggy and airless, he is too hot.

In the first case, when the pony is obviously cold, it may help to put on a lightweight rug which will prevent him from standing cold all night. Make sure that he has a good, deep bed.

When the pony breaks out in a cold sweat he may be wet or only slightly damp down each side of his neck and on each flank, but you must warm him and dry him again. Give him a good rub down with a handful of straw, pull his ears to warm them, and take him for a short walk outside the box. If it is not raining, this will dry him off. Putting on a lightweight rug when the pony is quite dry may help and should also prevent him from breaking out again that night.

With an over-hot pony, try to get some more air circulating around the box. If it is not raining, lead him out in the open and walk him about to cool off. A fuggy box is a menace.

The only way to find out what action to take is by trial and error, and by observation of each particular pony. Some just hate standing in, and they fuss and fret all the time. Others do not mind *where* they are. Unlike horses, ponies vary enormously in how they react to being in a stable.

The next morning – the earlier the better – half fill the water bucket, give the pony a good feed, and shovel up the droppings.

Pick out the pony's feet. Brush off any dry mud and caked droppings. Brush the mane and tail. Wipe him over with a rubber. In other words, groom him as you would after catching him up out of the field when he is dry.

10
Trimming, Washing, Clipping

A pony needs a good mane and a full tail for protection in winter and in summer, but this does not mean that they should become bedraggled and neglected. A good thick, even mane, not too short, will not lie sodden on the pony's neck; it dries out more quickly and is easy to keep brushed out.

A good forelock helps to protect the eyes from flies in the summer (*fig. 43*).

The tail needs little or no pulling, for it must be good and full all the way down. It does need the end banged: i.e. squared off (*fig. 44*). Too long a tail with the end trailing in the mud and the hocks never dry is a sorry sight and is no help to the pony's comfort or to his tail carriage. On the other hand, a tail well off the ground will dry out more quickly and will be much easier to brush out. In summer an over-long tail will soon become thin and wispy.

Both mane and tail, trimmed once in November or December, should keep in good shape throughout the winter when the hair is growing very little. In spring and summer they may need some trimming and tidying two or three times, according to how fast the hair grows.

A well kept mane and tail are easy to plait at any time.

In winter a pony needs the hair on the fetlock and down the back of the pastern and heels for protection. But in summer the pony will look smarter if these are trimmed.

With some ponies the old hairs of the fetlock and pastern come out quite easily by plucking with thumb and finger when they are changing their coat. Otherwise this should be done with scissors and comb, which will keep the hair lying naturally; if done with hand clippers it always shows up and looks rough.

A pony uses his eyelashes and the whiskers on his muzzle as feelers in the dark. These should never be cut off – nor should the hair be cut from inside the ears because it is needed for protection against weather and flies.

43 A good forelock helps to protect the eyes from flies during the summer.

Washing.

For a special occasion, and in warm weather, it is quite all right to wash the mane and tail or the whole pony. *Do not wash often, as washing removes natural oil and grease which is the pony's protection against, sun, flies, rain and wind.* For the same reason use soap and

59

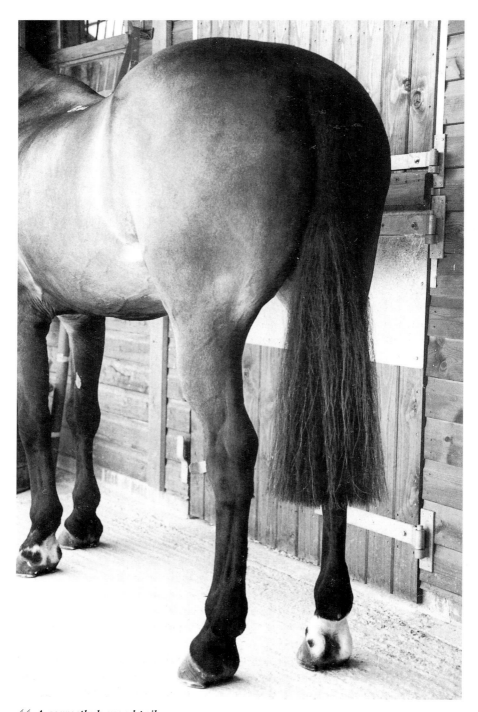

44 A correctly banged tail.

not a detergent. Soap leaves a little natural grease, whereas detergent removes too much. Never scrub legs to remove mud, as it cakes the pores of the skin.

When washing the whole pony, do it in a corner out of the wind. Have everything you will need ready *before* you begin. Use water that only just has the chill off it. Never use hot water.

Put a halter on the pony. Tie him up or ask someone to hold him. Have ready one bucket of tepid soap-suds, a piece of soap, and a sponge. Either a dipper or a small old saucepan with a handle are excellent for pouring the soapy water and the water for swilling over the pony. Several pieces of towelling are recommended for drying. Also needed are three buckets, each two-thirds full of tepid water, and one bucket of hot water. (The hot water is for adding to the tepid water which chills rapidly. The pony can thus be washed and rinsed in water which is all the same temperature).

Wash the head only if you must, and keep it as dry as possible, taking great care not to let any soap get into the pony's ears and eyes. Then, sponging and washing as you go, do the neck, mane, and so on, all over the pony's body, legs and tail. Use extra soap on very dirty patches and on the mane or tail. Rinse the pony over very throughly, getting out all the soap. Use a sweat scraper on the neck and body to remove surplus soap, and again after rinsing.

Drying the pony quickly is important, to prevent a chill, Dry the ears and loins well. Remove the worst of the wet from the rest of the body and legs. Make the pony move about as soon as possible, leading him around in the sun, if it is shining, but out of the wind.

If there is difficulty in getting the pony completely dry put some hay or straw on his back and loins and cover it with a rug and roller. When the pony is absolutely dry and warm, put on a summer sheet, or a light rug, and roller, and leave him in a stable set fair with clean straw. He is sure to roll.

If you have any doubts about being able to get the pony dry because of bad weather, don't wash him.

Clipping

Most ponies grow a heavy winter coat. When worked, they sweat profusely and get very thirsty. Unnecessary sweating makes them lose condition.

If the pony is going to do any work in the winter the kindest thing is to trace-clip him. When ridden he will not then feel his coat so much; he will sweat less; and he will dry off more quickly. The four types of trace-clip are shown in *fig. 45*.

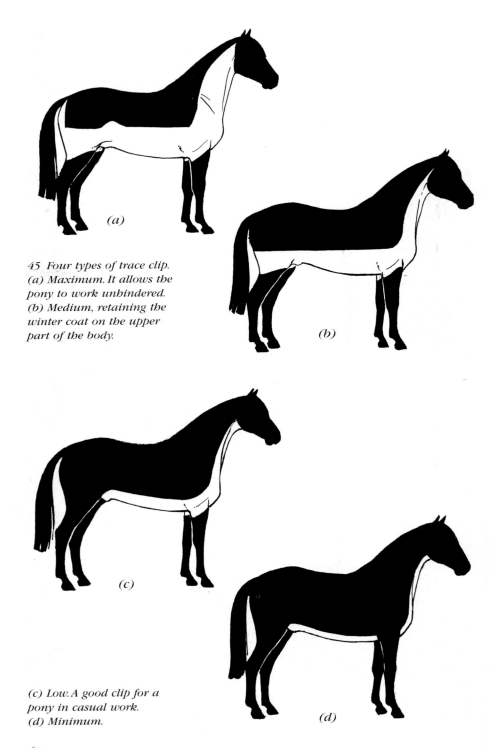

45 *Four types of trace clip.*
(a) Maximum. It allows the
pony to work unhindered.
(b) Medium, retaining the
winter coat on the upper
part of the body.

(c) Low. A good clip for a
pony in casual work.
(d) Minimum.

When clipped trace-high, ponies will come to no harm out at grass providing that the clip is not exaggerated by having too much coat removed along the sides and quarters, or up the gullet. One clip should be enough. If it is done at the end of November or in early December, the pony will be accustomed to it by the time that the very cold winds and weather begin. Also, a certain amount of, but not too much, coat will have grown again.

46 Stables set fair:(above) with straw, (below) with wood shavings.

11
The New Zealand Rug

This is a blanket-lined weatherproof rug with special fittings to prevent it from blowing about *(fig. 47)*. It can be used on a clipped pony who is going to be ridden regularly throughout the winter. The pony can be clipped with a hunter clip *(fig. 48)* and turned out in a New Zealand rug. One clip will be enough and it should be done in November or early December. The pony will then get used to the loss of his coat and will have grown a small amount of coat before the severe weather and cold winds set in.

Careful attention must be paid to the following points:

1.The rug should be tried on and the pony should be made much of and led about a few times before the rug is needed for regular use. The straps are in unaccustomed places and may frighten a pony if the rug is put on and he is turned out without some preparation.

 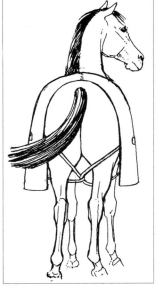

47 (Left) A pony wearing a New Zealand rug (Right) Diagram showing leg straps.

2. The rug must be fitted well forward on the withers. The breast buckle must be fastened high and short enough to prevent the rug from working back behind the point of the withers.

3. The leg straps should be passed through each other between the hind legs before being loosely fastened round the thighs.

4. The rug must be taken off and put on again carefully *at least once every day.* The ideal way is to have two rugs, one on and one off: then all the straps can be kept well oiled; the rug can be properly dried; the blanket lining kept brushed and clean; and the whole rug kept in satisfactory repair.

5. A daily check should be made of the points where the rug fits closest, to look for chafing and galling. Immediate steps should be taken to deal with any hurt. Never stand the pony in a stable with a New Zealand rug; as it is waterproof it is thick and heavy and allows no air to the pony's body, but is like wearing a mackintosh indoors. When the clipped pony has to stand in, put on a canvas or other type of stable-rug *(fig. 49)* of suitable weight, depending on the weather and on the pony's coat. Modern turnout rugs are of lighter weight, and although they may not be as hardwearing as the original canvas ones with blanket linings, they don't have leather straps (which need maintaining) and they don't become heavy when wet.

6. After a day's hunting the pony must be turned out into his field as soon as possible (see *'After a long day',* page 54). Extra care must be taken to remove mud where the rug, surcingle and straps touch, to prevent chafing. Dry the back and loins first, then keep them covered with a couple of sacks or a rug, putting straw underneath if the back is still damp. Then groom the rest of the pony. Avoid having him standing

48 A hunter clip.

49 A pony wearing an indoor (stable-) rug.

around getting cold: a clipped-out pony can get chilled very quickly. Finally, put on the New Zealand rug.

A pony clipped out and turned out in a New Zealand rug needs a generous extra ration daily of warming and energy-making food (i.e. coarse mix or pony cubes). It is important to remember that the rug is NOT a complete substitute for the pony's natural coat. Therefore if the pony is to keep his condition, he must be given much more food to help him maintain his body warmth.

12
Minor Ailments and First Aid

For full details, see the *Injuries and Ailments* section of *The Manual of Horsemanship*. A pony at grass should be looked over daily for wounds or illness, Lack of proper and immediate care may have serious consequence.

It is a good plan to have a definite method of running over the pony, doing it the same way each time. Then nothing will be overlooked. Knowing a pony's habits is a help in detecting if anything is wrong: i.e. when and where he usually lies in the field, how and where he often stands, etc. As a rule, ponies are tough and hardy and certainly do not want pampering. Given a little thoughtful daily care they will work on happily for years. It is no credit to any owner if his or her pony is continually having things wrong with him so that he is unable to be worked. Do not blame the pony.

Medicine Cupboard. The following is a list of recommended items which should always be on hand:
1. Blunt-ended scissors, to trim hair from around a wound.
2. A thermometer, either digital or mercury.
3. At least one roll of clean cotton wool, for cleaning wounds.
4. A commercial antiseptic solution, for cleaning wounds. The best contains chlorhexidine and should be available from your vet as Hibiscrub. An alternative is povidone iodine. (Pevidine scrub).
5. Non-adherent dressings to apply to wounds (e.g Melolin gauze) available from your vet.
6. Gamgee, to wrap around a leg before bandaging, or clean Fibagee, or other soft conforming bandage, e.g Soffban.
7. Clean, nonstick bandages, e.g. crepe bandages or stable bandages.
8. Sticky bandage, e.g. Vetwrap or Elastoplast.
9. Roll of adhesive tape.
10. Animalintex poultice.
11. Epsom salts, for tubbing a foot.
12. A clean bucket.

It is not necessary to have:
1. Wound powders or creams.
2. Hydrogen peroxide.
3. Liniments.
4. Colic drench.

It is essential to inspect the contents of jars, bottles, etc, regularly and to throw away anything that is stale.

Detecting Illness. You can tell when a pony is ill by the fact that he is standing with his head down and his ears back, and his coat is staring. His stomach will be tucked up and he will look thoroughly miserable.

The first thing to do is to lead him to a box or shed and send for the veterinary surgeon. In the meantime, pull the pony's ears to warm them – they are sure to be cold.If he is wet, rub him down, put some straw or hay over his loins then a rug, blanket, or sack. In any event you should cover his back and loins with a rug or sack. Offer some hay and water. Put some straw or other bedding on the floor of the box.

Coughing

This must not pass unheeded: it may be the first indication of trouble to come. It is wise to consult the vet before the trouble develops into something serious.

Out on a ride, if the pony gives an occasional dry-sounding cough it may be just a bit of dust or he might want to clear his wind. Note whether he coughs more than a couple of times.

If the cough has a wet thick, gurgle sound, and if the pony is not breathing correctly, seek advice.

If there is hardly any cough but the pony's nose is running – seek advice.

Do not work a pony with a persistent cough.

Whatever the cough, the pony is better out in the open air and not in the stable.

Ponies who are over-ridden or galloped too much may develop a cough and may, in time, become broken-winded. This is because the stomach, as it is full of grass, presses on the diaphragm and restricts the expansion of the lungs which are already having difficulty in keeping up with the too violent exercise.

Lameness

This can be noticed when the pony walks, but more often when he trots. Examine each shoe and under each foot. *Feel* for heat on feet and limbs.

For a suspected kick or blow, see the treatment described on page 73, for *Lumps*.

Very slight sprains, twists and wrenches will usually right themselves in a day or two if the pony is kept out in the field and not worked. Using the garden hose to trickle cold water over the affected area for twenty minutes two or three times a day will help.

Bad sprains need skilled attention.

There are many other reasons for a pony being lame. It is not practical or possible to go into them here. Skilled advice on the spot is necessary.

Usually a lame pony is better out in his field than standing in a stable getting stiff.

Avoid turning a lame pony sharply.

A lame pony **must not be worked**.

Ringworm

This is highly contagious, and it also affects humans as well as horses and ponies. It shows on the skin in circular patches (about the size of a fifty-pence piece) from which the hair pulls away. If you notice any unusual patches on your pony, consult your vet at once. Meanwhile, isolate the pony and all his tack and equipment. Do not groom him. Thoroughly wash you hands before contact with other people or animals. Thoroughly disinfect the stable, tack, and equipment before using them again for another pony.

Laminitis *(fig. 50)*

This is a fever in the feet due to intense congestion of the sensitive structure lining the walls of the hoof. It is a serious disease and is very painful, as the foot cannot expand to allow for the swelling. Ponies are particularly susceptible to it.

It affects all four feet – never a single foot. The pony will stand on his heels with his forefeet thrust forward, and be very reluctant to move.

It is caused by: too much food and not enough work; too much heating food, particularly when the horse is stabled; too much lush spring grass, especially with fat horses; too much trotting on the roads; or fast work on hard ground.

It is most important to consult your vet, but meanwhile stand the pony in a stable with plenty of bedding, so that he can lie down; and give him fresh water and hay. Do not feed hard food. In future, limit his access to grass and hard food, as he may be susceptible to further attacks. His feet must be regularly trimmed. by the farrier. Laminitis is potentially very serious, so prompt treatment in the early stages is essential

50 A pony suffering from acute laminitis.

Sweet Itch

This chiefly affects mountain and moorland types of pony in spring and autumn, causing the ponies to rub hair off their manes and tails. It is a very tiresome complaint, not unlike eczema in dogs, and is very itchy. As it is in the bloodstream, it can only be kept in check and not cured. Avoid rich grazing and any kind of food which might overheat the pony's blood. There are many soothing ointments and lotions available for dealing with this ailment.

Teeth

Have your pony's teeth inspected once a year by your vet or or a qualified horse dentist. Tooth troubles are fairly easily put right, and sharp edges can be removed by rasping, which the vet or dentist will do for you.

Thinness
This may be caused by any of the following:
Not enough to drink.
Not enough to eat.
Not enough bulk food.
Poor quality food.
Sharp teeth.
Worms.
Bullying by other ponies. (See page 74).
Temperament.
An illness.
(The first four have already been dealt with under *'Grazing'* and *'Feeding'*).

Thrush
Dirt, lack of proper care of a pony's feet, and thrush, go hand in hand. A pony is not usually troubled with thrush if his feet are regularly picked out, and attended to by the farrier at proper intervals.

Thrush can be smelled when a pony's foot is lifted and picked out and the cleft of the frog becomes slimy. Having picked out the feet, wash them thoroughly. Next, the dead tissue has to be cut out of the affected area – for which you will need your farrier. Then, with Stockholm tar (which can be bought at most tack and pet shops, and chemists) and a short, stiff brush, paint all over the heels, sole and frog, penetrating well into the cleft and grooves. This treatment must be carried out daily until the thrush is cured.

Worms
All ponies harbour worms and will never look fit and well unless they are kept under control by a regular programme of treatment. Your vet will advise you as to what dose to use and at what intervals.

Cuts and Wounds
The size of cut does not necessarily reflect its severity. A small superficial graze can be managed by clipping the surrounding hair and then cleaning thoroughly. Any larger wound, a wound with severe bleeding, a deep puncture wound or any wound close to a joint, a tendon-sheath or a tendon, or a wound on the. back of the fetlock or pastern, should be examined by a vet, who will assess whether vital structures may have been damaged, and whether or not the wound needs stitching (suturing). If in any doubt call the vet.

To clean the wound Clip, or trim with scissors, the hair surrounding,

71

the wound, so that hairs do not lie in it. Wash the wound with clean water from a clean bucket, preferably using an appropriate antiseptic solution – chlorhexidine (Hibiscrub), or povidine iodine (Pevidine). Soak small wads of cotton wool in the warm water. Squeeze the water out; water dripping down the horse's leg may frighten him. Pour some antiseptic solution on to the cotton wool and rub the wound. Repeat with multiple clean pieces of cotton wool, continuing for at least five minutes, or longer if the wound is not clean. If the wound is very dirty wash it with a hose first. Careful and thorough cleaning will help to prevent infection.

Do not apply wound ointments or powders, because these may make dirt stick and attract infection. Superficial small cuts will heal quickly if the wound edges are close together. If possible, apply a non-stick dressing and then bandage the wound.

Keep the horse in a stable if you can, because the wound will heal more quickly if the edges are not moving continuously, and it is easier to keep the wound clean. It may be necessary to use a fly repellant around (but not in) the wound if the horse is out at grass and it is not possible to keep the wound covered.

Check vaccination status. If the horse is fully vaccinated against tetanus, further treatment is not required, but if it is more than a year since the horse was vaccinated, or if the vaccination status is unknown, it is essential to call the vet. who will treat the horse with tetanus anti-toxin and a booster vaccination. Tetanus is a potentially life-threatening complication of any wound.

Puncture wounds can be dangerous because the surface cut may be small, but it is difficult to assess their depth, and bacteria are often pushed deep into the tissues. These wounds are therefore difficult to clean thoroughly.

If there is any chance that the wound is near a tendon or a joint, or on the back of the pastern, you must call a vet as an emergency. If the wound is not near any of these structures, a poultice is generally advisable and may help to clean it, but your vet may need to give antibiotics to control deep infection.

Large cuts will probably heal quickest if the wound edges are brought together using stitches or staples. The final cosmetic result will also be much better: the amount of scarring will be reduced.

A bruised area may benefit from cold poulticing for 24 hours, to help to reduce painful swelling. After this period it is necessary to increase the circulation to the area to help to remove the inflammation. This is best achieved by gentle movement. The exception may be if there is a wound that has been sutured (stitched), since movement may disrupt wound healing. Your vet will be able to advise you about this.

Girth and Saddle Galls
The majority of galls are caused by poor management, due to either dirty or illfitting tack. A string girth may cause pinching and bruising, especially if the horse or pony is overweight. A girth gall is a painful swelling in the girth region. Sometimes there is hair loss and possibly an open sore. If the skin does become broken, wash it with a weak antiseptic solution. Application of surgical spirit may help to harden unbroken skin. The tack must be thoroughly cleaned and checked to ensure that it is correctly fitted. A tubular synthetic or a leather girth is less likely to cause a problem than a string or nylon one. Do not use the saddle again until the galls are completely healed.

Insect Stings
These can cause big, soft lumps anywhere on the body, which usually go down on their own in a few hours. A sting on the eyelid or near the eye can be bathed **very gently** with cold water or cold tea.

Lice
These usually trouble ponies at grass in the spring. They can easily be seen if the hair of the mane or tail is parted. If allowed to infest the pony they will cause bare patches on his mane, tail, back, neck or withers. Though lice are infective to other ponies, they are not serious and can easily be treated under veterinary supervision.

Lumps
Lumps with heat in them will be sore and bruised, as will a cut from a blow, kick or tread. Use the garden hose to trickle cold water **very gently** from well above, so that the water flows and spreads over the sore area *(fig. 51)*. Alternate with Kaolin applied as for thorns, described below.

Thorns
A wound from a thorn should be treated as a puncture wound. *(See Cuts and Wounds)*. Bathing with warm water will soothe the affected area, which must be kept clean and allowed to heal from within. If there is noticeable swelling, your vet may need to give antibiotics to control the infection.

51 *Cold-hosing a pony's sore legs and feet.*

Other Problems

Bullying. Sometimes a pony is bullied by another in the field. As he therefore never gets a chance to settle and graze, he becomes worried and loses condition. The only remedy is to remove either him or the bully from the field.

Temperament. A pony who frets, fusses, sweats easily, breaks out, or rarely seems relaxed when being worked, is not easy to keep big and well.

Vaccination. It is important to follow guidelines which are fully explained in the 'Prevention of Disease' section of *The Manual of Horsemanship* (Chapter 33).

13
Companionship

52 Companionship,

Where possible it is beneficial to turn out two ponies together *(fig. 52)*. In the winter they protect each other. In the summer they stand head to tail to help keep off the flies.

One pony turned out on his own can be very lonely. In summer he can have a very bad time with the flies, and in winter with the wind and rain.

14

Bringing in a Pony in Summer

Flies are worse in some districts and fields than in others. Ponies walk a tremendous distance in a day trying to avoid them; also they will gallop if flies are very bad. Bringing a pony into a cool, airy box or shed for a few hours will save him a good deal of discomfort and much wear of his joints, feet and shoes.

The pony may be in the stable from about 10 am until 5 pm, which is a long time with no food. So give a small mid-day short feed or a small net of hay. Be sure that there is always a bucketful of clean water in the box.

For the following two reasons (and there are others) there must be bedding on the box floor – not necessarily expensive straw; any dry litter will do.

1. The pony will want to stale during the time that he is in his stable. Few ponies will trust themselves to do this unless there is enough bedding to prevent them slipping.

2. If there is bedding the pony will lie down during the day, which is good for him. He will not have much time for rest when turned out in the evening because he will be busy eating. It is cruel to stand any pony for long in a stable with little or no bedding.

Treat the pony as a stabled pony for the time he is in: that is, keep the droppings picked up, the water bucket topped up, and the box tidy.

After the pony is turned out in the evening, set the box fair so that it is all ready for him the next day.

Ponies have conservative habits, and sometimes they are shy drinkers. It may be that a pony will not always drink from a stable bucket. Do not be misled into thinking that he never drinks very much. Watch him when he is turned out. He will either go straight to his usual drinking place, or after a roll and a mouthful of grass he will trot off to drink.

15
Riding a Pony off Grass

Most ponies thrive when worked off grass, but the following three points are worth noting:

1. Although a pony's feet and legs get plenty of walking exercise when at grass, they do harden up – so ride on the side of the road or on the grass verge. Avoid riding in the middle of the road or on a hard road unless it it absolutely necessary. When riding on verges, look out for cans and bottles in the long grass, and for open drainage ditches alongside hedges

2. A pony's back muscles, where he carries his saddle and his rider, get out of practice for bearing weight. It is in his loins that he gets tired. Therefore **never sit on any pony unnecessarily**, nor for too long. When his back starts to get tired he may trip, brush, stumble, refuse to jump or not jump well. He may pull, and be blamed for all sorts of other things, when all he is trying to do is to ease tired muscles.

3. A pony gets out of the habit of having a long day's work whether hunting, working rally or competition. He will become tired and thirsty even if his rider does not. Many a pony, young and old, gets soured by continually giving of his best while his rider never knows when to call it a day. So when possible, at *all* convenient times, give the pony a short rest, a short drink at a trough or stream, and a few mouthfuls of grass. This has no harmful effect and will go a long way towards keeping the pony fresh and warding off fatigue.

So, briefly, to sum up the needs of the pony kept at grass:

- Fresh clean water always.
- Shelter from flies and wet,windy weather.
- To be caught up and looked over every day.
- A strong gate and good fences.
- A visit to or from the farrier every four to six weeks.
- Hay every day from November to May.
- Some extra feed in hard weather.
- A change of grazing.
- Another pony for companionship.

The pony kept out to grass, though out of sight, needs just as much care and forethought as the stabled pony, who is continually under one's eye.

Finally, in everything to do with ponies at all times remember these three words:

ALERTNESS   ANTICIPATION   COURTESY

53 *'Keeping a pony at grass'*.

Index

Illustration page numbers are in italic

Ailments, 24, 67-74

Bandages, 48, 49, 72
'Banging' tail, 58, *60*
Bark, eating, 11
Beans, 25
Bedding, 56, 68, 76
Bran, 32
Bullying, 19, 74

Care of ponies.
  after long day, 53-55
  after short ride, 53
  after stabling overnight, 56/7
  before fitting New Zealand
  rug, 65/6
  before stabling overnight, 56
  the day after work, 55
  when wet, 50-51, 54/5, 61
Catching ponies, *41*, 41-44
Chaff, 25, 32
Clipping, 61-63
  hunter clip, 64, *65*
  trace-high 61-63, *62*
  when to clip, 63
Coarse mix, 26, 32, 66
Coats, ponies changing, 19, 45
Cold, catching, 56
Coughing, 68
Cubes, 25/6, 32, 66
Cuts, 71/2

Droppings, picking up 13, *14*

Ears, 56/7, 68
Electric fences, 13, 17, *18*

Farrier, 38, *38/9*, 40, *54*
Feed and feeding, 25-35, 66, 76
  after grooming, 51
  cost of, 32
  extra, when New Zealand rug
  worn, 66
  extra, caution needed, 28
  in frost and snow, 36, *36*
  'short' feed, 25, 32

small ponies, 26, *26*
storage of feed, 32, *33*
table of quantities, 29
trough for feed, *33*
when to feed, 28-30
yearly pattern, 30
Feet, 37-40, *37-39*
  ailments and faults 68-69, 71,
  74
  care of when grooming, 48-
  50, 53
  farrier at work on, *39*
  in frost and snow, 36
  inspecting, *53*
Fences, 16-19, *17*, *18*
  electric, 13, 17, *18*
  post-and-rail, *17*
Fetlock, 58
Field shelters, *19*, *20*
Fields, 11-24
  inspecting, 21-23
  overgrazed, *13*
First aid, 67, 71-73
Flies, 75/6
Forelock, 58, *59*
Frost and snow, 36

Gates, 16/17, *16*
Girth galls, 73
Grass, 11-13, *12*
Grazing, 11-13
  area needed, 24
  area per pony, 24
Grooming, 45-52, *50*, *52*
  after work, 53-55
  dry ponies, 48-49
  equipment, 45, *46*
  wet ponies, 50-52, *50*
  why necessary, 45

Halter, 42, *42*, 55, 61
Hay, 25, 32, 35
Haynets, 30-31, 34, *34/35*
Headcollar, 42, *43*
Hedges, 13, *14*, 17, 19, *21*
'Horse-sick' fields, 11, *13*
Hunter clip, 64, 65
Hunting, 54, 56, 65

Illnesses, 24,67-74
Insect stings, 73
Inspecting,
   after work, 55
   feet and shoes, *53*,55
   fences, 19

Lameness, 68/9
Laminitis, 24,69,*70*
Lice, 73
Loneliness, 75
Lumps, 73

Maize, 25/6
Mane, 57,58,59-61
Manual of Horsemanship,40,67
Medicine cupboard 67/8

New Forest ponies, *9*
New Zealand rug,*64*,64-66
Nuts, pony *see* cubes

Oats, 25,26,27

Patting, 44
Poisonous plants, *22/3,* 23
Ponds 15
Ponies,
   regular feeding,28
   shy, 41
   shy drinkers, 76
   summary of needs, 77
   temperament, 74
   too cold or too hot, 56/7
   tying up, 45,*47*
   very small, *26*
   when not to ride,55
   when not to
   stable, 53,54
   wild, 9-10

Red worm, 11
'Remove', 38
Riding off grass,77/8
Ringworm, 69
Risen clenches,37,*38*
Roads, 77
Rubbing against posts etc, 19

Rubbing down, 50,*50*
Rug, New Zealand, *64*,64-66
   daily checking, 65
   fitting,65

Saddle, 50
Salt, 11
Sheds, 19,*19*
Shelter, *19,20,21*
Shoes, 37-40,*38/39*
Snow and frost, 36
Sprains,68/9
Stables and stabling 56/7,76
Stocking, 24
Sweating, 56/7,61
Sweet itch, 70

Tail, 57,58,59-61
   correctly banged,*60*
   washing, *52*
Teeth, 70
Temperament, 74
'Thatched' ponies,
   50,51,*51*
Thinness, 71
Thorns, 73
Thrush, 71
Trace clip, 61-63,*62*
Trimming, 58
Turning out, 43/4,*44*
Tying up ponies, 45,*47*

Vaccination, 74

Washing, *52*,59-61
Washing wounds,71-72
Water, 15-16,*15*
   pond, 15
   stream, 15
Water troughs, 15-16,*15*
   in icy weather, 36,*36*
   suitable, *15*
   unsuitable, *15*
Weeds, 11
Welsh ponies, *10*
Worms, 71
Wounds, 71-72